The Great Escape

by Peter Millett
illustrated by Alfredo Belli

CAMBRIDGE
UNIVERSITY PRESS

UCL
Institute of Education

Every summer, Selma and her family went to the beach for their holidays.

Selma's brothers loved to go swimming in the sea, but Selma didn't.

She felt much safer on the land.

'Come on, Selma,' Dad cried. 'Maybe you can go in the water this year? You're much bigger now.'

'No, I'm staying here on the beach,' Selma said, shaking her head.

One day, the wind in the bay was very strong. It made the sea choppy and rough.

Out of the blue, a whale came swimming into the shallow waters.

'Look!' Selma cried. 'A whale!'

'Cool ...' Selma's brothers rushed into the water.

Dad looked alarmed. 'This bay is no place for a whale,' he said quietly.

Daren and Zami swam out towards the whale.

'He must be coming to play with us,' Daren shouted.

'This is amazing,' Zami laughed. 'We are so lucky to see a whale!'

Dad frowned. 'No, we're not lucky. This could be
a big problem.

Whales aren't meant to come in this close to land.'

Selma jumped up and pointed at the horizon. 'Look, look!
There are more whales coming into the bay!'

6

Dad shook his head and began to look very worried.

Daren and Zami watched as the first whale swam right past them and headed towards the sand.

'Where's it going?' Zami cried.

The whale ran aground just a few metres away from Selma.

'Huh? Why did it do that?' Selma asked.

'It's lost,' Dad said. 'It's badly lost.'

'Look!' Daren shouted. 'There are even more whales.'

The bay filled with whales, swimming in all directions. Daren and Zami quickly paddled back to the beach and jumped out of the water.

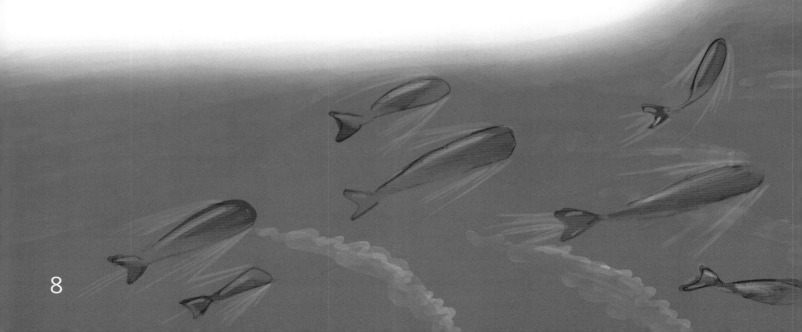

9

Two whales beached themselves next to the first one.

'Oh no,' Selma cried. 'Now they're all starting to get into trouble.'

Dad grabbed his phone and called the police.
'Send help right away,' he boomed. 'The bay is filling up with beached whales!'

Soon, six whales had beached themselves on the sand.

'Quick,' Dad shouted. 'We have to stop the sun burning their skin. Cover them with wet blankets.'

Daren and Zami grabbed some blankets and dipped them in the sea.

They threw them over the shaking whales. Everyone on the beach helped.

Selma poured her bottle of water over one whale's head to keep it cool.

'How do we make them swim back out to sea?' Selma cried. 'Whales can't swim backwards, can they?'

Dad wiped his brow. 'We'll have to wait until the tide comes right back in. Then we'll turn them around and push them back out to sea.'

Selma frowned. 'Do we have to go into the water with them? I don't want to!'

'Yes,' Dad said.

Selma shook her head. 'I don't think I can do that,' she said.

Dad smiled. 'Selma, you might be scared of the water, but the whales are more scared of the land. I need you to be brave to help them.'

Selma went quiet.

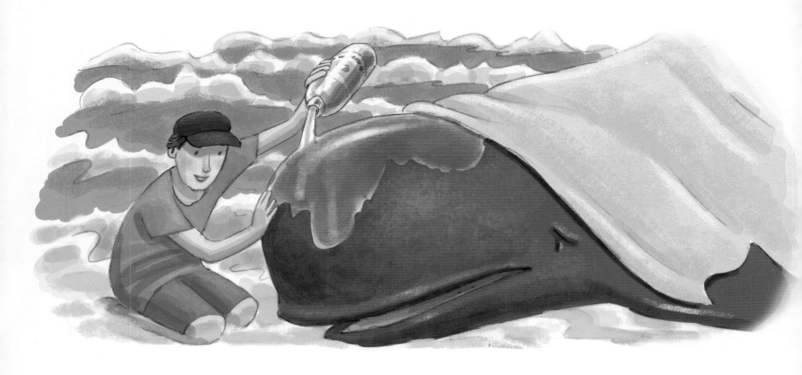

After a little while, the police came down to the bay.

They brought more helpers with them.

Everyone worked hard to try to keep the whales cool and protect them from the sun.

16

A few hours later, the tide came all the way back in.

Everybody rushed to help the whales back to sea.

Selma took in a deep breath and stepped into the sea next to a whale.

The whale she was helping looked distressed.

'Selma! Don't let the whale see you're scared,' Dad said. 'Just look into its eyes with your brave face. If you are brave, the whale will be brave too.'

Selma kept staring into the whale's eyes as the water rose up to her knees and then to her waist. 'Everything's going to be okay,' she whispered to the whale.

Selma held her breath as the water rose up to her chest.

SPLOSH! The whale flapped its tail and started swimming back out to sea.

Selma beamed as she watched it swim away.

'Good girl. You did it!' Dad cheered. 'You helped save a whale.'

Before Selma could say anything, Daren called out to her.

'Hey, Selma! I need your help!'

Selma waded over to her brother and helped him push out another whale.

Then after that, Zami called his sister to come over and help him, too.

Selma smiled to herself as she watched whale after whale being rescued from the beach.

Dad hugged his brave daughter.

'So, do you like both the land and the water now?' he chuckled.

Selma smiled at her Dad. 'Yes,' she said. 'I like both now. But it's much calmer being on the land!'

The Great Escape Peter Millett

Teaching notes written by Sue Bodman and Glen Franklin

Using this book

Developing reading comprehension

In this story, it is the whales that make a great escape after becoming beached. The story deals with how Selma overcomes her personal fear of the water to help save the whales. 'The Silk Road' and 'Yu and the Great Flood' are examples of texts that also deal with overcoming adversity.

Focusing on specific words and phrases and discussing how they influence the messages and meanings the reader gets will help develop reading comprehension at a high level.

Grammar and sentence structure

- Amount of direct speech requiring use of punctuation to read fluently and with expression.
- Literary phrases; *'Out of the blue; as she watched whale after whale...'*
- Adverbial phrases

Word meaning and spelling

- Challenging vocabulary; *'beached', 'aground', 'choppy', 'boomed'*
- Decoding polysyllabic words: *'horizon', 'distressed', 'directions'*
- Inflection –er; *'safe/safer', 'calm/calmer', 'big/bigger'*

Curriculum links

Science – Activities flowing from this text include: the harmful effects of the sun; the power of water; sea mammals. All of these topics could lead to research to write information books that could be shared as class texts.

PSHE – How we overcome things that we are frightened of could lead to some creative and reflective writing either on themselves or familiar story characters. For example,

children's picture books, such as 'The Owl who was afraid of the Dark', 'Can't you sleep Little Bear', 'Curious George goes to the Hospital' and 'The Gruffalo' could be shared as starting points to creative writing.

Further reading in Cambridge Reading Adventures that links to the ocean include: 'Life on the Reef', 'Giants of the Ocean'.

Learning Outcomes

Children can:

- take more conscious account of literary effects used by writers
- solve most unfamiliar words on-the-run by blending less common digraphs and recognizing alternative spellings to read longer and more complex words
- read silently or quietly at a more rapid pace, taking note of punctuation and using it to keep track of longer sentences.

A guided reading lesson

Introducing the text

Give each child a copy of the book and read the title.

Orientation

Give a brief orientation to the text: *This book is called 'The Great Escape'. Take a look at the cover; who or what do you think is escaping? Why do you think that?*

Preparation

Page 2: *Selma and her family are on the beach, but Selma doesn't go in the water – why do you think that is?*

Page 4: *Here, the sea is described as 'choppy and rough' – find those words in the text. What do you think those*